CHESTER and CARRAWBURGH IN THE DAYS OF THE ROMANS

by
FRANK GRAHAM

Illustrated by
Ronald Embleton

I.S.B.N. 0 85983 117 5

1979

2nd Edition 1985

Published by Frank Graham, 6 Queen's Terrace, Newcastle upon Tyne, NE2 2PL

Printed by Howe Brothers (Gateshead) Limited

CHESTERS FORT— CILURNUM

The name Chesters is found frequently in Northumberland applying to fortified sites especially those of Roman origin. Symeon in 1104-8 calls the place *Scytlescester juxta murum*. If we have the correct place Allen Mawer says the modern name should be Shittleschester and the original owner would be one *Scytel*. The Roman site here is of great interest. Beside the fort itself we have the finest military bath-house in Britain, remarkable remains of a Roman bridge and a museum with an outstanding collection of Roman antiquities discovered at various places on the Wall. With a few exceptions the museum is the work of John Clayton (1792-1890) a wealthy man who was deeply interested in the Roman remains to be seen in the neighbourhood of his home. The Reverend Thomas Machell in 1691 was the first writer to record the fort. Hutchinson (1778) says this was the first station in his tour "where the direct appearance of regular streets was observed," the place being "crowded with the ruins of stone buildings." He also recorded many ruins to the south of the fort and some to the north. The *Notitia Dignitatum* gives us the Roman name of Cilurnum.

Cilurnum was garrisoned by a cavalry regiment *ala II asturum*, the Second Asturian Horse — 500 strong. Benwell, a similar fort, was occupied by the First *ala*. The fort measures north to south 582 feet and east to west 434 feet, covering $5\frac{3}{4}$ acres. It is the customary rectangle with rounded corners and six gates. The wall is 5 feet thick backed by an earthern mound and fronted by a ditch.

At Chesters the northern rampart does not coincide with the wall as at Housesteads. It lies across it just as at Benwell (Condercum) and Rutchester (Vindobala). This was normal in cavalry forts.

The Gateways

The gateways at Chesters were all of the same type. Our reconstructions of the main gateway the *porta decumana* (page 15) shows what they were like. The double gate has towers on either side with guard chambers. The *spina* separating the two portals is built of massive masonry. The rest is in stone similar to the wall itself. The doors would be of oak reinforced with iron. The doorways of the guard rooms opened into the gate-passage.

North Gate (Porta Praetoria)

The visitor enters the fort by this gateway. It is a double portal gateway but its west portal was blocked very early since its threshold is almost unworn. Its east portal however is of great interest since the stone channel of an aqueduct enters here, fed by one of the springs to the north of the fort.

Main West Gate (Porta Principalis Sinistra)

This also has twin portals and guard chambers. However, both sills are unworn suggesting the gate was walled up at an early date. The northern guard chamber has a large stone storage tank fed by an aqueduct to the west. Whether there were one or two aqueducts we don't know but the bringing of water (aqua adducta) is recorded in an inscription (to be seen in the Museum) probably of the early third century when the governor was Ulpius Marcellus. The Narrow Wall on a broad base comes up to the south tower. Originally the wall crossed the fort and in 1945 Turret 27a was found near the north east corner of the headquarters building.

Smaller West Gate (Porta Quintana Sinistra)

About 50 yards to the south is a single portal gateway with little to be seen. Travelling round the fort we meet traces of the angle tower and half-way between the angle and the south gate is a fine interval tower. The doorway at the back led on to the street called the INTERVALLUM. The gutter can still be seen. There were eight interval and four angle towers at Chesters. They were all probably raised 10 feet above the rampart walk like the gate towers.

South Gate (Porta Decumana)

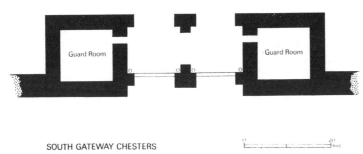

Guard Room

Guard Room

SOUTH GATEWAY CHESTERS

Has the usual twin portals and towers. The western portal was blocked when still new. The eastern portal was restored on more than one occasion, after the fort had been overrun, so the level of the portal is much higher. In the east guard chamber of this gate a remarkable bronze tablet of 146 A.D. was found. It is a *diploma* or *tabula honestae missionis*.

This was given to an auxiliary soldier when he had served for twenty-five years and received an honourable discharge. It legalised his marriage past or future. The original is in the British Museum but a copy can be seen in the Chesters Museum.

The strongroom (aerarium). Woodcut showing its aspect
when discovered.

3

Smaller West Gate (Porta Quintana Dextra)

Of the eastern wall only the gateways can be seen. This gate is a single portal and the MILITARY WAY, leading from the bridge across the Tyne, enters the fort here.

Main East Gate (Porta Principalis Dextra)

In a fine state of preservation with walls standing twelve courses high. It was never used by wheeled traffic and was walled up about 300 A.D. Each portal had an arch at back and front and the south near pier still has the slots on top of the upper course which held the shuttering for the arch.

Headquarters (Principia)

This is the most important building in the fort, almost twice the size of that at Housesteads, and the finest on the line of the Wall. It was the nerve centre of the fort. Here in the various rooms all the business of the regiment was transacted. The entrance was on the north through a monumental gateway (although there are two side entrances as well) into an open courtyard. From here the visitor could look straight ahead through the Cross Hall to the chapel. The courtyard was paved with a veranda on three sides whose supporting columns can still be seen. In the north west corner is a well and nearby on one of the paving stones is a large phallus. From the courtyard the spacious Cross Hall is entered. The south side is occupied by five rooms. The central one is the *sacellum* which housed the regimental colours and a statue of the emperor. The chapel gave access to the strongroom which was under one of the rooms of the standard bearers. It was used for the money and valuables of the regiment. The two rooms to the west of the chapel were the offices of the adjutant who controlled the regimental records. The two rooms to the east were used by the standard bearers who looked after the company records and the individual savings of the soldiers. The strongroom (*aerarium*) is illustrated here from an old woodcut. It was found by accident in 1803 but only excavated in 1840. We are told that "a tradition existed in the country that the station had been occupied by a cavalry regiment and that the stables, which were capable of accommodating 500 horses, were underground. The rustics when they came upon this vault naturally enough thought that the later part of the legend was about to be verified and that they would soon enter the stables; it was not to be so, however. An oaken door, bound and studded with iron, closed the entrance into the chamber, but it fell to pieces shortly after being exposed. On the floor were found a number of base denarii, chiefly of the reign of Severus. The roof of the apartment is peculiar. It consists of three separate arches, the intervals between them being filled up by the process called 'stepping over'."

Commandant's House

This building is very confusing but was obviously an elaborate and luxurious house with the normal Roman central heating and a private bath-house attached. The commander of a cavalry unit (*praefectus equitum*) was a man of importance in the Roman army.

There were probably two granaries to the west of the headquarters but the area has not been excavated. The fragments of a large building to the south of the Commandant's house probably contained the regimental hospital.

The civil settlement was to the south and east of the fort. Excavations have not been carried out but aerial photography suggests there was a large population here with several important houses. Excavations at some future date will probably provide valuable information about civilian life on the frontier. The vicus here was almost a military town.

Chesters Roman Camp Reconstruction

WILLIAM HUTTON AT PLANETRESS

When we visit the Roman Wall today we find that large sections have been demolished. Most of the demolition was deliberate. The stone was needed for road construction and farm buildings. The greatest destruction took place in the 19th century. When William Hutton visited the Wall in 1801 he saw the process taking place. When he came to Planetress, a mile east of Chester, he intervened to try and halt the removal of a fine section. Ronald Embleton has tried to recapture this famous incident as described by William Hutton.

"At the twentieth milestone I should have seen a piece of Severus's wall $7\frac{1}{2}$ feet high and 224 yards long, a sight not to be found in the whole line: but the proprietor, Henry Tulip, esq., is now taking it down to erect a farm house with the materials. Ninety-five yards are already destroyed, and the stones fit for building removed. Then we come to 13 yards, which are standing and overgrown on the top with brambles. The next 40 yards were just demolished, and the stones, of all sizes from 1 pound to 2 cwt., lying in one continued heap, none removed; the next 40 yards are standing 7 feet high.

Decurion and troopers of a cavalry *ala*, 3rd century A.D.

Then follows the last division, consisting of 36 yards, which is sacrificed by the mattock, the largest stones selected and the small left. The facing stones remain on both sides. This grand exhibition must be seen no more. How little we value what is daily under the eye.

Here was a fine opportunity for measuring. The foundation was, in fact, below the surface of the ground and consisted of two courses of stones, each 6 inches thick, extending to the width of $6\frac{1}{2}$ feet. The second course set off 3 inches on each side, which reduced the foundation to 6 feet, and the third 3 inches of a side more, reducing the wall to $5\frac{1}{2}$ feet, its real thickness here.

The foundation is laid in the native earth, the bed is cemented with mortar. The soil being afterwards thrown up on each side of the Wall 2 feet high caused the foundation to be 3 feet deep.

I desired the servant, with whom I conversed, to give my compliments to Mr. Tulip and request him to desist, or he would wound the whole body of antiquaries. As he was putting an end to the most noble monument of antiquity in the whole island, they would feel every stroke. If the wall was of *no* estimation he must have a mean opinion of me, who would travel 600 miles to see it; and if it *was* he could never merit my thanks for destroying it. Should he reply 'The property is mine and I have a right to direct it as I please', it is an argument I can regret but not refute."

Ronald Embleton

The Stables and Barracks

Cavalry regiments were divided into 16 units called *turmae* and each consisted of 30 men commanded by a decurion, and two N.C.Os. Ronald Embleton's reconstruction (page 6) shows a decurion with two troopers of an *Ala* in the third century. Almost nothing is known of the stables at Chesters apart from their sites which are partially conjectural. Since there were at least 500 horses in the fort and since in the winter they would consume large quantities of hay and straw it is difficult to visualize how they could have been accommodated in the eight blocks suggested for stabling. (It is noteworthy that the cavalry fort of Hunnum had to be increased in size).

Some of the barracks can, however, be seen. Cavalry were given more ample accommodation than infantrymen, probably because they kept their harness and equipment where they slept. There were eight barrack blocks. Each housed two *turmae* and at the ends near the fort walls were the rooms of the unit commanders. The 60 men were probably equally divided among the remaining ten rooms. The barracks had a veranda on which the cooking was done. Some of the pillars which supported this veranda can be seen.

When Ronald Embleton painted the interior of one of the barrack rooms he was faced with many questions—Were there racks for weapons? Did the Roman cavalryman store his saddle and bridle in the stables or did he keep them with his belongings in the barrack room? Cloak, mail shirt, tunic, breeches, eating utensils, helmet—there had to be a place for all these articles. How did the Roman soldier sleep? Wrapped in his cloak? Did he have a mattress, blankets? Did he have single beds or two-tiered bunks? Was the barrack room cluttered and squalid or was it rigidly organised?

Archaelogical discoveries have provided NO answers to any of these questions. There was no hard evidence only conjecture. The drawing of the barrack interior is the most important in the book. Imagination based on common sense has furnished us with an intelligent answer to the questions that were posed.

9

Bath-house

The large military bath-house outside the fort is one of the sights of Chesters. Due to the damp air and changes of heat bath-houses needed constant attention to prevent deterioration. The bath-house at Chesters has undergone several alterations. So today it is difficult to follow exactly the route the bathers would take through the various rooms.

They entered by a flight of steps from the military way leading to a porch which gave access to the Dressing Room. This was the largest room in the baths as was customary. Going to the baths was a social function where you met friends and had a chat, almost like a club, so this main room needed to be substantial. In the west wall are seven niches. Their use is a matter for argument. Alcoves for statues, for clothes, for ointments, etc., have all been suggested. To the east of the changing room was a latrine. Leaving the main room the bather entered the vestibule. From here three rooms opened. On the left was the cold room with a washing basin in the centre. To the right were two rooms for dry heat, the inner one being the hottest. Straight ahead were the warm and hot rooms with moist heat. Off the hot room was a room containing a hot bath. This room was lighted by a window the broken glass of which was discovered when excavating. Parallel with the *tepidarium* and *caldarium* are two extra warm rooms entered from the cold room to the north.

The rooms were heated by a complicated system of hot air channels, which ran under the floors and through the walls, the heat being provided by three stoke holes.

To keep in the heat the various warm rooms had barrel vaulted ceilings composed of blocks of tufa, which were light and so avoided the necessity of heavy buttresses on the walls. The rest of the baths had the conventional roof of red tiles.

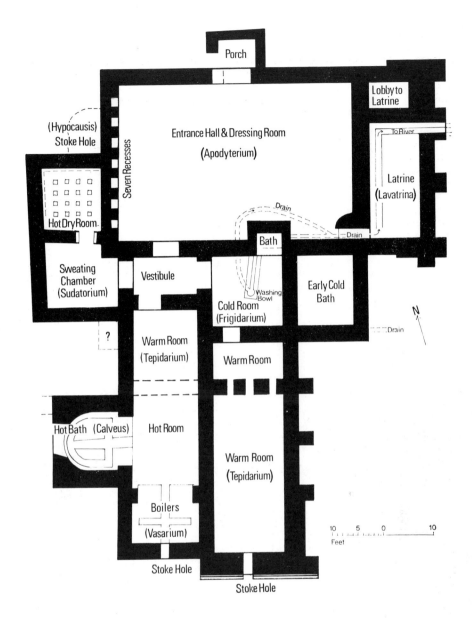

Porch

Lobby to Latrine

(Hypocausis) Stoke Hole

Entrance Hall & Dressing Room (Apodyterium)

Seven Recesses

To River

Latrine (Lavatrina)

Drain

Drain

Hot Dry Room

Bath

Sweating Chamber (Sudatorium)

Vestibule

Washing Bowl

Early Cold Bath

N

Cold Room (Frigidarium)

Drain

?

Warm Room (Tepidarium)

Warm Room

Hot Bath (Calveus)

Hot Room

Warm Room (Tepidarium)

Boilers

(Vasarium)

10 5 0 10
Feet

Stoke Hole

Stoke Hole

Roman Bridge

The remains of the Roman bridge at Chesters are an outstanding example of Roman civil engineering. The bridge had stone piers with a wooden superstructure. There have been two bridges on the site. The first was a narrow bridge arched in stone carrying only the Wall across the river. The second was wider and carried the Military Way. On the next page we show an early reconstruction by Paul Braion. Today his drawing would be changed in many ways (for example the drawbridge at the two ends would not be included) but Paul Brown was a pioneer in showing the Wall as it once was when the Romans were still here.

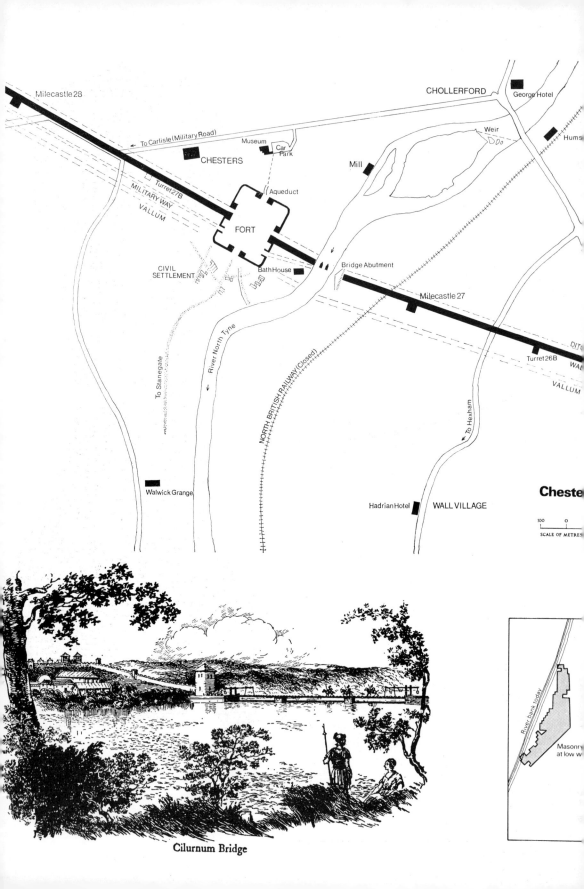

Milecastle 28

To Carlisle (Military Road)

CHOLLERFORD

George Hotel

Museum

Car Park

CHESTERS

Weir

Hums

Turret 27B

MILITARY WAY

Mill

VALLUM

Aqueduct

FORT

CIVIL SETTLEMENT

Bath House

Bridge Abutment

Milecastle 27

To Stanegate

River North Tyne

NORTH BRITISH RAILWAY (Closed)

Turret 26B

DIT

WA

VALLUM

To Hexham

Cheste

Walwick Grange

Hadrian Hotel

WALL VILLAGE

100   0

SCALE OF METRES

River bank today

Masonry
at low w

Cilurnum Bridge

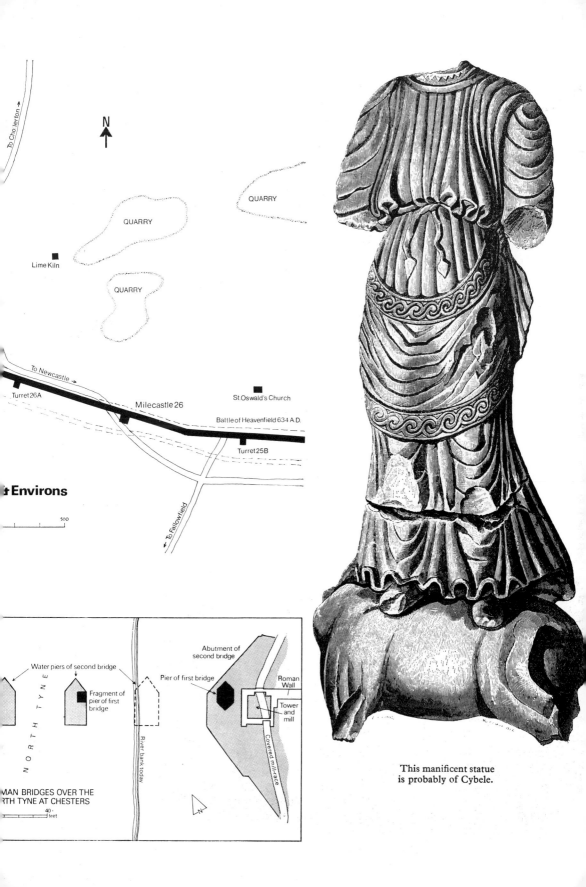

To Cho ler ton

N

QUARRY

QUARRY

Lime Kiln

QUARRY

To Newcastle

Turret 26A

Milecastle 26

St.Oswald's Church

Battle of Heavenfield 634 A.D.

Turret 25B

To Fallowfield

† Environs

500

NORTH TYNE

Water piers of second bridge

Fragment of pier of first bridge

River bank today

Abutment of second bridge

Pier of first bridge

Roman Wall

Tower and mill

Covered mill-race

N

MAN BRIDGES OVER THE
RTH TYNE AT CHESTERS

40
feet

This manificent statue
is probably of Cybele.

IN THE BATHS
AT CHESTERS

Donald Embleton

Reconstruction of the main gateway....*Porta Decemana*

The east gateway at Chesters in the
19th century

CHESTERS-CILURNUM

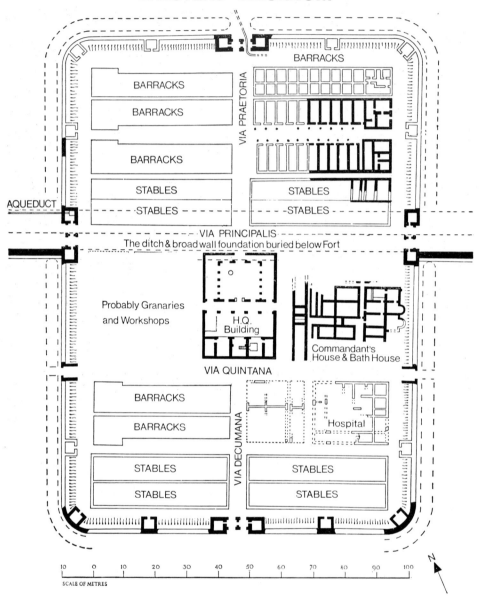

The Blacksmith's Shop explanatory plan. Labelled areas include:

BARRACKS, VIA PRAETORIA, BARRACKS, BARRACKS, STABLES, STABLES, AQUEDUCT, VIA PRINCIPALIS, The ditch & broad wall foundation buried below Fort, Probably Granaries and Workshops, H.Q. Building, Commandant's House & Bath House, VIA QUINTANA, VIA DECUMANA, BARRACKS, BARRACKS, Hospital, STABLES, STABLES, STABLES, STABLES

SCALE OF METRES
10 0 10 20 30 40 50 60 70 80 90 100

N

The Blacksmith's Shop

A blacksmith's shop would be essential in any Roman fort especially one used for cavalry. There would be the day to day repair of armour and weapons and the shoeing of the horses. Horse shoes were used by Roman cavalry but samples are not often found. We have therefore had to use a sample from the cavalry fort at Benwell.

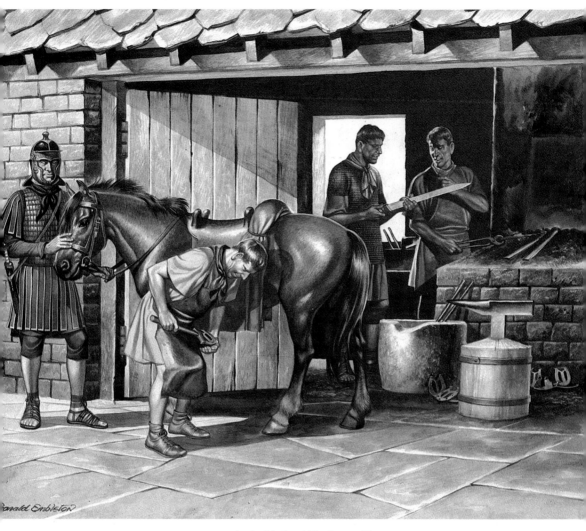

At the blacksmith's shop at Chesters

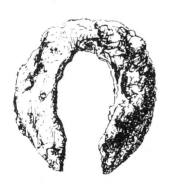

Roman horseshoe. This rare specimen was found at Condercum. There are also examples in the Museum at Chesters.

Relief of a signifer or standard bearer of the early 3rd century from the fort at Carrawburgh. Clayton Museum, Chesters fort.

From the book *What the Soldiers wore on Hadrian's Wall* by Russell Robinson.

The coloured plate show the equipment of the soldier reconstructed

opposite Roman officers from Chesters hunting wild boars.

THE TEMPLE OF MITHRAS AT CARRAWBURGH

Little can be seen of the Roman fort of Brocolitia but the religious remains are of great importance. So much has been found that it could almost be described as a religious centre although most Roman forts probably had as many temples but they have either not survived or have not yet been found. The most important temple found is the one to Mithras.

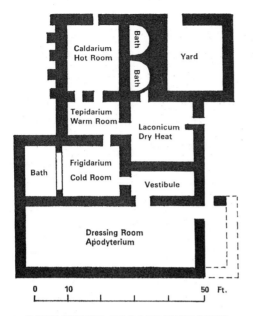

Caldarium
Hot Room

Bath

Bath

Yard

Tepidarium
Warm Room

Laconicum
Dry Heat

Frigidarium
Cold Room

Bath

Vestibule

Dressing Room
Apodyterium

0   10   50   Ft.

BATH-HOUSE AT CARRAWBURGH
Excavated by Clayton in 1873

CARRAWBURGH
(Brocolitia)

Little can be seen of the fort here which stands on a bare flat moor. The north rampart and the wall are covered by the road while the east, west and south ramparts are only mounds in the fields. It covers about three and a half acres. In the second century the garrison was the first cohort of Aquitanians, later the first cohort of the Cugernians and in the third and fourth centuries the first cohort of Batavians. Little excavation has taken place here although the walls would be impressive if cleared of debris. The position of the vallum is of great interest. It can be seen as though passing through the fort. Clearly the fort was built later than the vallum and was built over it. This makes Brocolitia either contemporary with or later than the Narrow Wall which formed the north rampart.

The western and southern slopes outside the fort were occupied by the *vicus* in which was a bath-house excavated by Clayton in 1873. In plan it was similar to the one at Chesters. Nothing can be seen of it today.

Outside the south west corner of the fort in boggy ground are the remains of the most important Mithraic temple to be found in Britain. It was discovered in 1949 during a very dry summer. Three altars to Mithras, still standing in positon, were seen protruding through the grass. The following year it was completely excavated. Building was early in the third century and alterations were carried out several times before its destruction in 297 A.D. It was rebuilt shortly afterwards but before many years had passed it was demolished early in the fourth century, probably by Christians.

The pilgrim entered the ante chapel (Nathex) by a door in the south wall. On his left was the hearth where food was prepared and nearby was the ordeal pit. To the right, in front of the wickerwork screen is the statuette of a mother goddess. On entering the nave raised benches could be seen on either side. Here were four small altars especially the twin statues representing on the east CAUTES (torch upright to represent the rising sun) and on the west CAUTOPATES (torch downwards to represent the setting sun). At the far end was the sanctuary with its three main altars dedicated by officers from the fort. The western one depicts Mithras as charioteer of the sun (dedicated to Marcus Simplicius Simplex), the central altar is dedicated by Lucius Antonius Proculus, and the eastern altar is dedicated by Aulus Cluentuis Habitus. Behind the altars in a recess would have been a relief showing Mithras slaying the bull, but it was probably destroyed by Christians. (The altars to be seen in the Temple are replicas. The originals are in the Museum of Antiquities at Newcastle University.) North west of the Mithraeum on the edge of the vallum is Coventina's Well. It was discovered in 1876 but had been recorded by Horsley in 1726.

"They discovered a well. It is a good spring, and the receptacle for the water is about seven foot square within, and built on all sides, with hewn stone; the depth could not be known when I saw it, because it was almost filled up with rubbish. There had also been a wall about it, or an house built over it, and some of the great stones belonging to it were yet lying there. The people called it a cold bath, and rightly judged it to be *Roman*."

21

Here was found the richest collection of Roman coins and altars ever discovered on the frontier. There were 13,487 coins (apart from many carried away in a raid on the site) and numerous altars and native objects now to be seen in the Chesters Museum. The water goddess worshipped here was the Celtic *Coventina*. The whole shrine measured forty feet square internally with the sacred spring in the centre. Among the coins found were over three hundred brass "*as*" of Antoninus Pius. They commemorated the pacification of northern Britain after the revolt of 155. They show Britannia sad and disconsolate with her head bowed unlike her usual portraiture.

Shrine of the Nymphs and the Genius Loci

The shrine was discovered in 1957 and excavated by Dr. D. J. Smith in 1960. The remains consist of a sandstone altar standing on a pedestal, a well and an apsidal stone structure. The altar is inscribed on back and front with the same words suggesting it stood in the centre of an open shrine to be read on both sides. The text is as follows:

NYMPHIS (E) T G(E)N(10)
LOCI · M · HISP(A)N(IV)S
MODESTINVS · P(R)AE(F)
COH · T · BAT · P(R)O SE
ET SVIS · L · M

The translation could be "To the Nymphs and the Genius Loci, Marcus Hispanius Modestinus, Prefect of the First Cohort of Batavians, willingly (dedicated this altar) on behalf of himself and family."

The side of the altar has a ladle and pole-axe carved on it. The apse is a problem since it is unlikely that it supported a roof. The *nymphaeum* was probably open to the air. The well itself, unlike that of Coventina, unfortunately contained no treasures.

The nymphaeum abuts on the mithraeum. The date of its construction is uncertain but it fell into disuse early in the 4th century.

(Article and reconstruction based on report by D. J. Smith in *Archaeologia Aeliana* 4.XL. 1962).

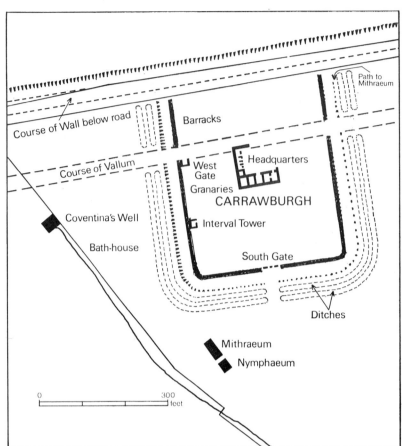

Course of Wall below road

Path to Mithraeum

Barracks

Course of Vallum

West Gate

Headquarters

Granaries

CARRAWBURGH

Coventina's Well

Interval Tower

Bath-house

South Gate

Ditches

Mithraeum

Nymphaeum

0   300 feet

JEWELRY WORN AT CILURNUM

Gem engraved with a scene represen a chariot race.

Engraved carnelian bezel of a ring. seated figure is thought to be Jupit

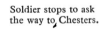

Soldier stops to ask the way to Chesters.